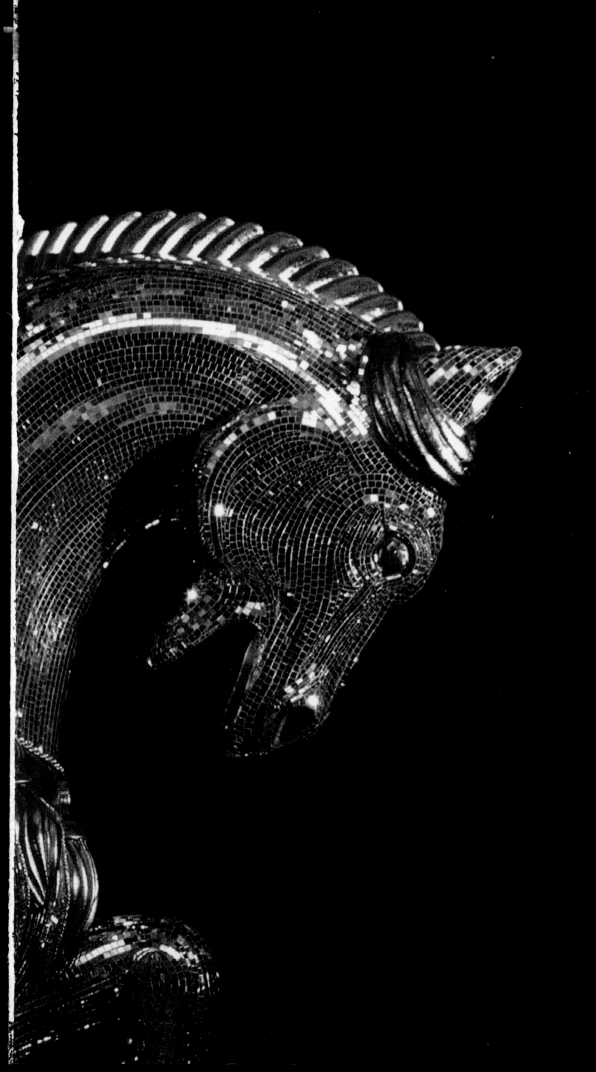

BELLAGIO

CONSERVATORY & BOTANICAL GARDENS

and other projects by

DESIGN SOLUTIONS

Cover Design and Composition by Dianne Stonecipher
Book Design and Composition by Dianne Stonecipher and Susan Tinkle
Cover Photograph by John Wadsworth, John Wadsworth Photography
Photography by John Wadsworth, John Wadsworth Photography
Plus City, Austria Photography by Helmuth Humphrey

First Printing 2010
Printed in China

ISBN 978-0-578-04181-0

Published by Design Solutions
2332 Irving Boulevard
Dallas, Texas 75207
www.designsolutions-usa.com

ACKNOWLEDGMENTS

Our special thanks to

Randy Morton, President and Chief Executive Officer, Bellagio Resort & Casino
Robert Stowe, Vice President, Engineering
Andy Garcia, Director of Horticulture, Bellagio

John Wadsworth Photography
www.johnwadsworthphotography.com
John has been photographing Design Solutions' installations for over thirty years.

Austrian photography by Helmuth Humphrey
Olympics photography by John Wadsworth Photography and Michael Desjardins

DESIGN SOLUTIONS

Stephen C. Stefanou

Design Solutions is the United States' premier design company for year-round and seasonal displays. Its president, Stephen Stefanou, has been in the design and display industry for forty years, and since founding this Dallas-based firm, he has become famous for his dazzling displays of monumental proportions. Working with a staff of brilliant artisans and technicians as well as creative experts from around the world, Stefanou's iconic displays become 'must-see' destinations. Among them are the 22-foot composition of giant red Chrstmas ornaments, the 30-foot holiday ornament emerging from the ground in front of the MGM Grand Detroit, and the towering gold leaf ornament tree for the Embarcadero Center in San Francisco. Other clients include American Express, Sony, AT&T, ExxonMobil, The Coca-Cola Company, Gaylord National, MGM Mirage, Sands Corporation, the Trump Organization as well as property management groups, municipal governments and private individuals.

In 2002, Design Solutions entered the Las Vegas market at the request of the Bellagio Resort & Casino's Conservatory and Botanical Gardens' horticultural director. This unique collaboration has continued. Five times a year the Conservatory at the Bellagio is transformed by Stefanou's extraordinary imagination. His original designs uniting the flowers of the seasons with handmade sculptures, topiary creatures, animation and whimsy are breathtaking. Among these now iconic displays are the impressive God of Prosperity and the magnificent mirror pavé Tang Dynasty horse for Bellagio's annual Chinese New Year celebration. Even its renowned spa has an icon: a 19-foot quartz obelisk, which is the world's largest rock crystal object.

During the 2010 Winter Olympics, Design Solutions created a spectacular display for Ocean Spray and the City of Richmond to celebrate its prolific cranberry industry. The Canadian Olympic Committee logo became a classic cranberry bog that was positioned adjacent to the O Zone, the official Olympic celebration site. The bog, nearly the size of a football field, was filled with 13,000,000 cranberries provided by Ocean Spray's owner/growers.

Over the years, Design Solutions has been recognized with awards of excellence to include First Place/Retail Centers award for the top retail project in the U.S and Grand Prize award for Top International Project.

HOLIDAY

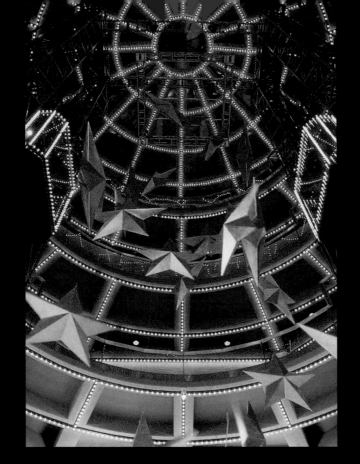

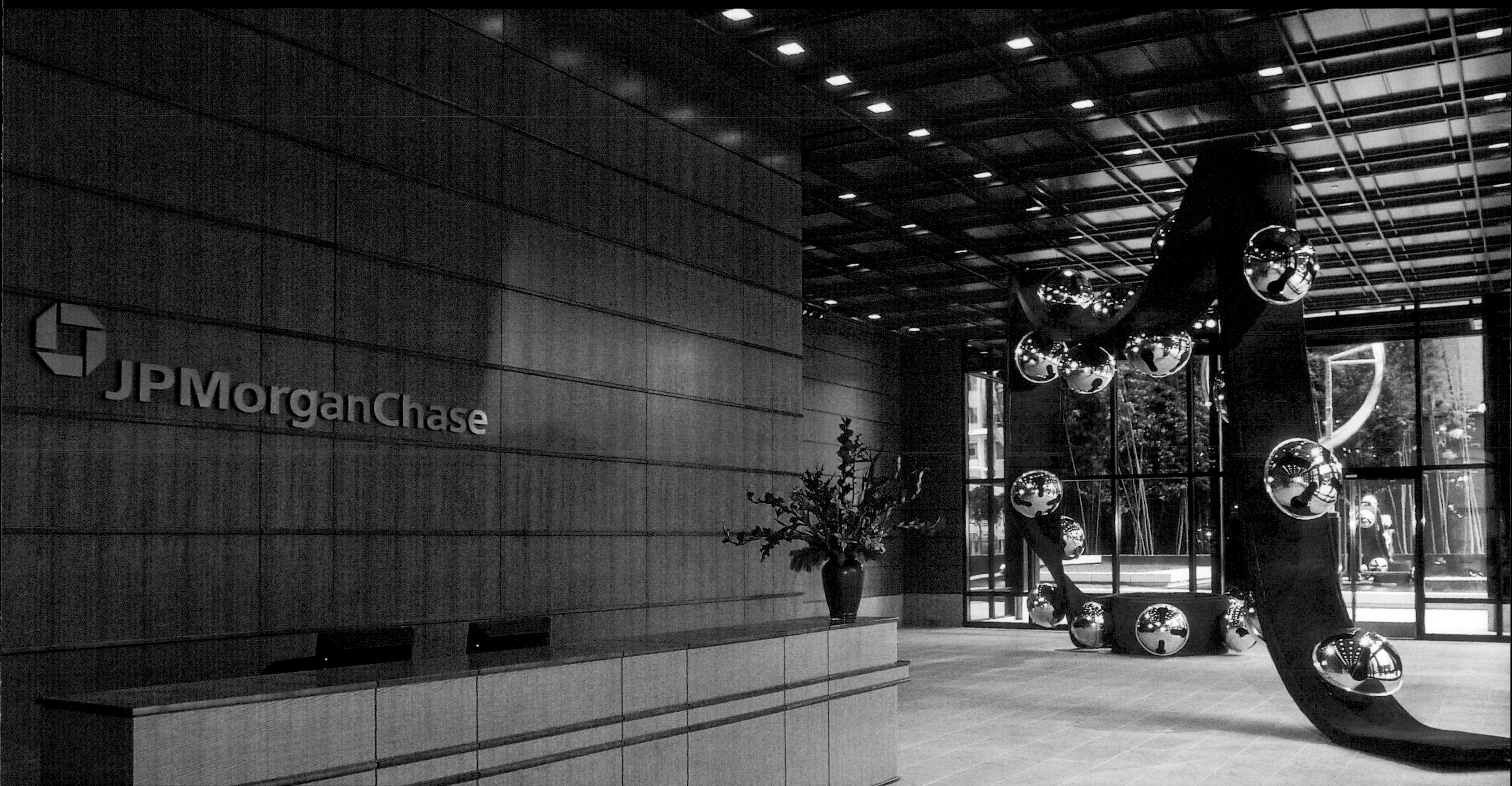
JPMorganChase

SPRING

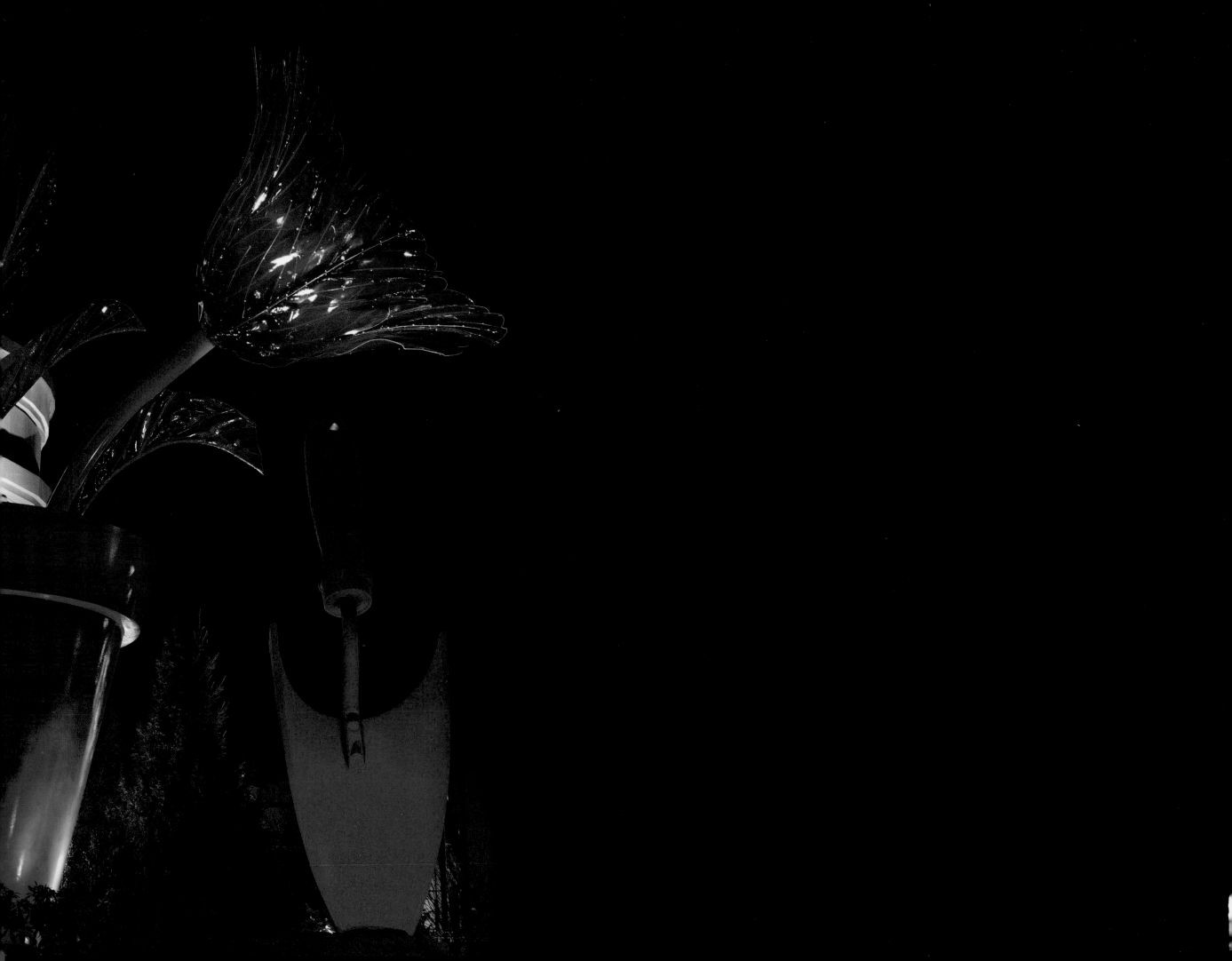

Everblooming Gardenia
Gardenia jasminoides 'Veitchii'

WEST
66

SUMMER

AUTUMN

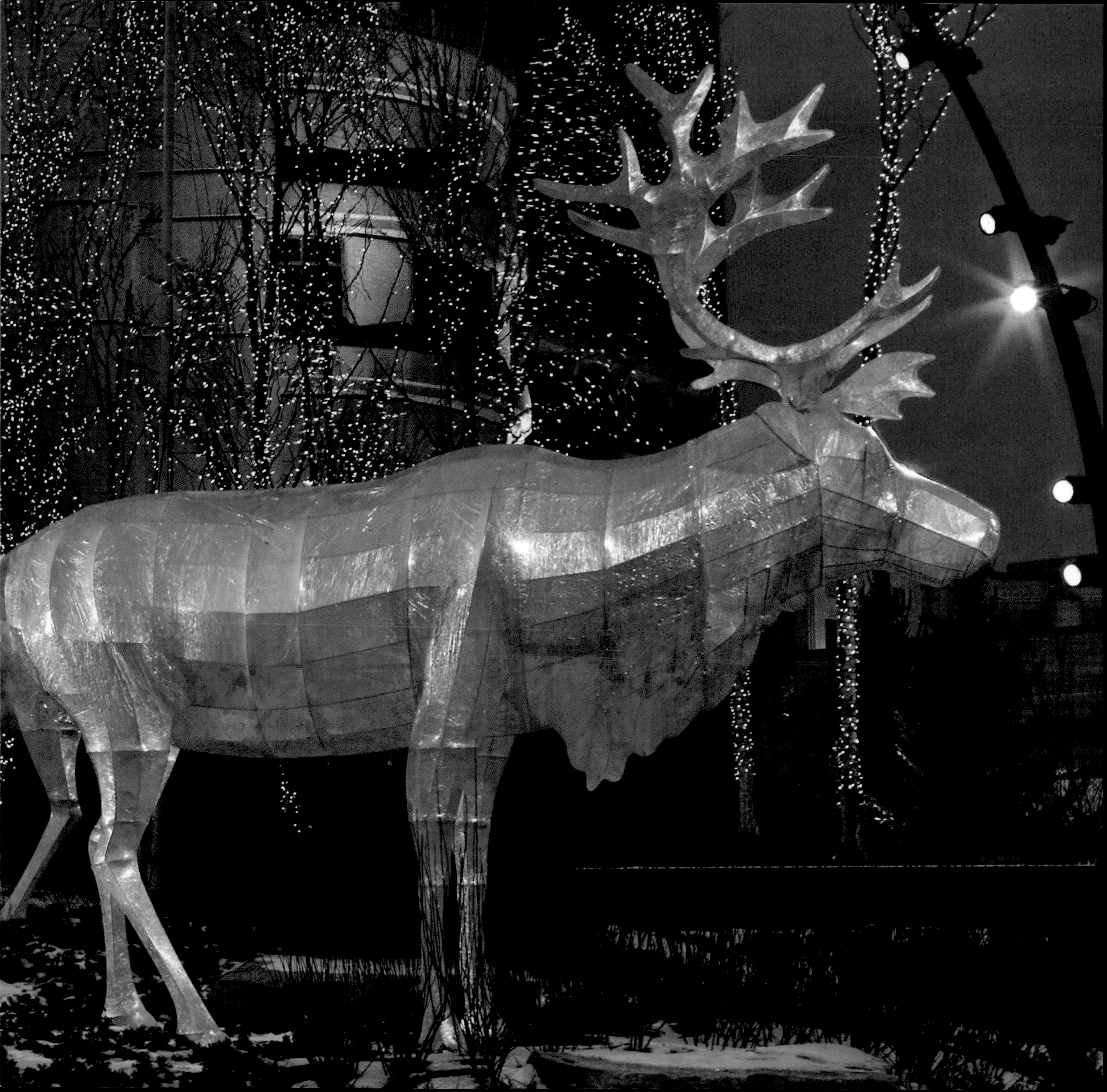

WINTER

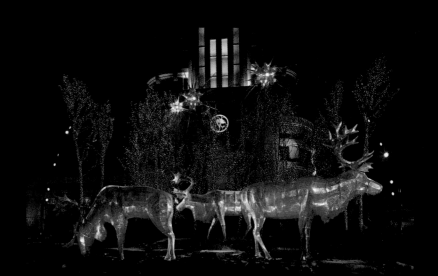

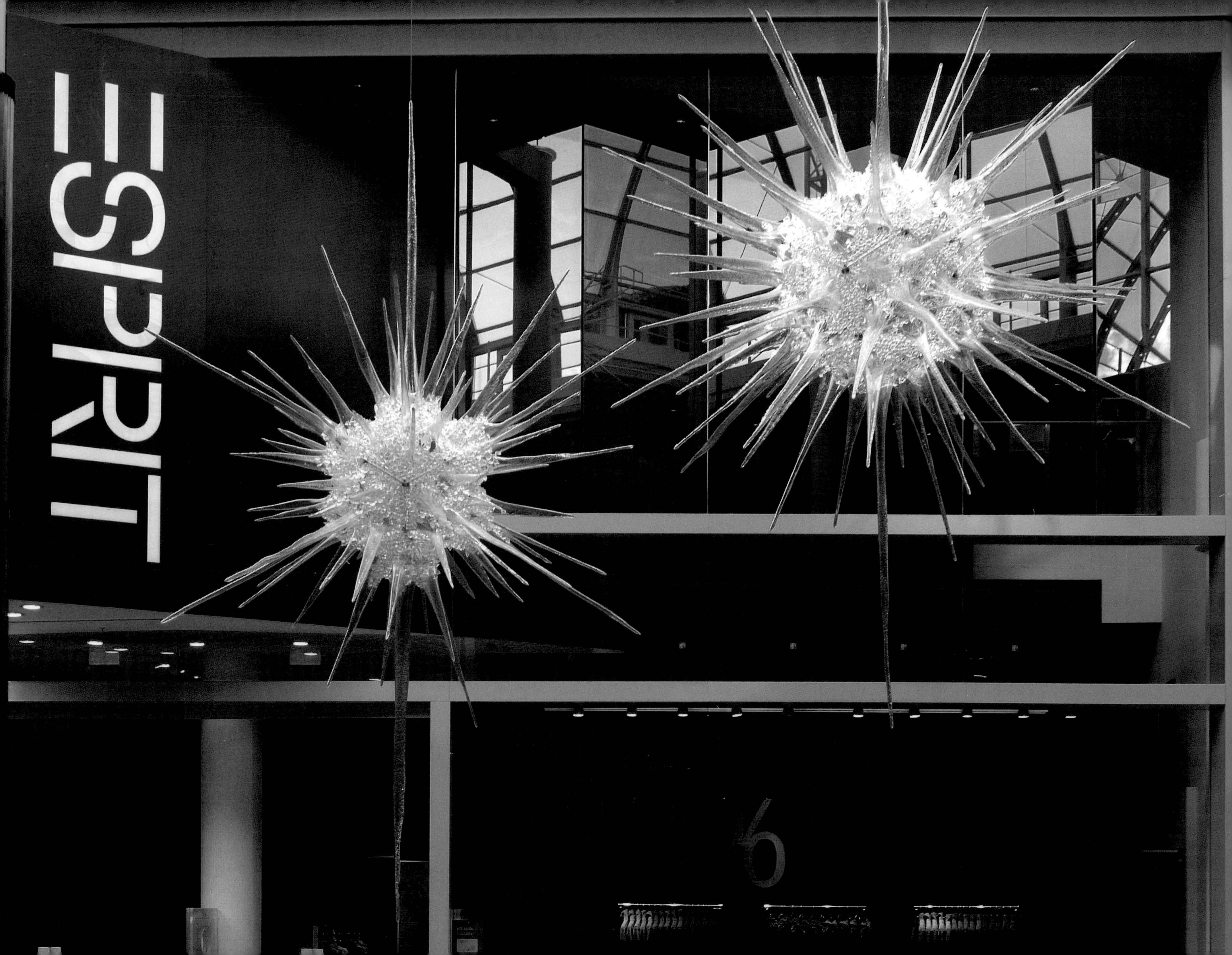
ESPRIT
6

CHINESE NEW YEAR

CAFE BELLAGIO

OLYMPICS 2010

For the 2010 Winter Olympics, 13 million cranberries were transformed into a 15-ton, 46,000-square-foot floating cranberry "bog" that forms the Canadian Olympic Committee's logo of five intertwined Olympic rings and giant maple leaf containing a gold-leaf Olympic flame. The bog was filled with Richmond-grown cranberries provided by Ocean Spray grower-owners, harvested in October and November and frozen until placed into the giant bogs. The City of Richmond is the heart of Canada's cranberry country and home to more than 60 family-owned farms, most of which are part of the Ocean Spray Cooperative. Cranberries are also known as "wonderberries" for their significant health benefits, which perfectly complement Olympian athleticism.

More than 6 months went into the creation of this amazing display, from original artist's renderings of the concept to final installation. The company took what cranberries do best as an artistic medium — float — and used them to create a stunning one-of-a-kind visual display. The installation was visible from nearly one mile in the air, creating an iconic image for visitors to the 2010 Olympics.

After the Olympic Games, the cranberries were composted to nourish future crops.

CLIENT LIST
(SELECTED)

American Express World Headquarters, New York
Bellagio Resort & Casino, Las Vegas
Boston Properties, Embarcadero Center, San Francisco
Boston Properties, Prudential Center, Boston
Castle Casino, Atlantic City
Century City Shopping Center, Los Angeles
City Center, Las Vegas
City of Burbank, Burbank
City of Richmond, British Columbia, Canada
City of Rowlett, Rowlett, Texas
Coca Cola World Headquarters, Atlanta
Compass Management, 787 Seventh Avenue, New York
Copley Place, Boston
Corporate Property Investors, Lenox Square Mall, Atlanta
Cushman and Wakefield, Nations Bank Tower, Dallas
Duke Energy, Charlotte
Equitable Tower, New York
Exxon World Headquarters, Irving, Texas
Faberge USA, Inc., New York
Fashion Show Mall, The Rouse Company, Las Vegas
Faison Stone, Williams Square, Irving, Texas
First Union Plaza, Wachovia One, Two & Three, Charlotte
Gaylord National Resort, National Harbor, MD
Grand Hyatt, New York
Hahn Company, San Diego
Henry S. Miller Company, Dallas
Hines Interests, 101 California, San Francisco
Hines Interests, 222 Berkeley, Boston
Hines Interests, 500 Boylston, Boston
Hines Interests, 225 West Wacker, Chicago
Hines Interests, Norwest Center, Minneapolis
Hines Interest, 50 Fremont, San Francisco
Hines Interests, 31 West 52nd Street, New York
Hines Interests, 450 Lexington Ave., New York
Hines Interests, 505 Montgomery, San Francisco
Hines Interests, 560 Mission, JPMorgan Chase, San Francisco
Hines Interests, 601 California, San Francisco
Hines Interests, 885 Third Avenue, New York
Hines Interests, 1100 Louisiana, Houston

Hines Interests, IDX Tower, Seattle
Hines Interests, Renaissance Tower, Detroit
Hunt World Headquarters, Dallas
John Buck Mgmt Company, Leo Burnett Agency, 35 West Wacker, Chicago
Koll, Chemical Plaza, Chicago
Konover Property Trust, Mt. Pleasant Towne Center, Mt. Pleasant, SC
LCOR, Inc, Chicago Title and Trust Company, Chicago
Lowe's Anatole Hotel, Dallas
MGM Detroit Hotel & Casino, Detroit
Maguire Thomas Partners, Southlake/Solana, Roanoke, TX
Mall of America, Minneapolis
Mary Kay World Headquarters, Dallas
Miglin Beitler, Chicago Mercantile, Chicago
Mirage Casino & Hotel, Las Vegas
Mitsui Fudosan, Inc., New York
NorthPark Center, Dallas
Norwest Plaza, St. Louis
Ocean Spray Cranberries, Inc.
Panache, Atlanta
Plus-City, Austria
Premisys Real Estate Services, Prudential Plaza, Chicago
Red Development: Village Pointe Shopping Center, Omaha
Republic First National Bank, Midland, TX
Radio City Music Hall, New York
Rockefeller Center, New York
Sony Corporation, New York
Southcoast Plaza, Costa Mesa
Stein & Company, AT&T Corporate Center, Chicago
Trammell Crow Company, Dallas
TI (Treasure Island) Hotel & Casino, Las Vegas
Trump Organization, New York
Trump Plaza, Atlantic City
Union Station, Washington, D.C.
Urban Retail Properties, Copley Management, Chicago
Urban Retail Properties, Oakbrook, Oakbrook, IL
USAA Headquarters, San Antonio
USAA, Norfolk
Venetian Resort & Casino, Las Vegas
Westin Hotel, Dallas
Zales Corporation, Dallas

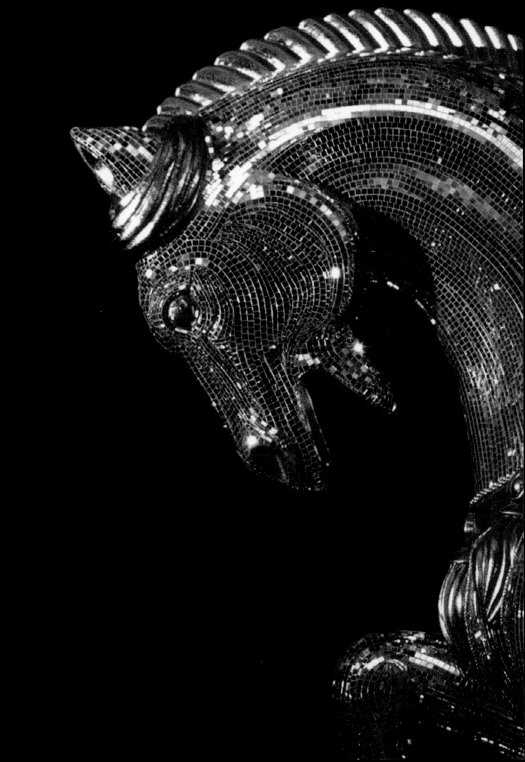

FOR INFORMATION, PLEASE CONTACT

Barbara Petricini Buxton
2332 Irving Boulevard
Dallas, Texas 75207

Phone: 214-871-0801
Fax: 214-954-1086
Barbara@DesignSolutions-USA.com

HOLIDAY

HOLIDAY

1-2 MGM GRAND DETROIT, DETROIT, MICHIGAN

Large (30-foot diameter) emerging Holiday Ornament of steel-reinforced fiberglass with red metal flake finish and hand-applied silver leaf 8-foot diameter cap. Thousands of white LED mini-lights adorn the surrounding 50-foot Birch forest.

3 BELLAGIO, LAS VEGAS, NEVADA

A Cranberry Bog of 1,400 pounds of fresh cranberries supplied by Ocean Spray, floats on a rectangular pond in which rest four topiaries, each containing 4,000 fresh red roses. A topiary Papa Bear of 28,000 white carnations watches from the side.

4 BELLAGIO, LAS VEGAS, NEVADA

50-foot Holiday Tree featuring custom-sculpted four-foot Acanthus leaves finished in hand-applied gold leaf, mirror pavé balls and custom ornamentation. Tree is topped with an 8-foot gold leaf Millennium star and surrounded by 8- to 18-foot holiday ornaments decorated with velvet, hand-applied gold leaf, and jewels.

5 BOSTON PROPERTIES / PRUDENTIAL CENTER, BOSTON, MASSACHUSETTS

Detail of Ornament showing hand-applied gold leaf, mirror mosaic tiles, jewels and holographic applique.

6 BOSTON PROPERTIES / PRUDENTIAL CENTER, BOSTON, MASSACHUSETTS

Suspended from the atrium ceiling are 5-and 8-foot diameter steel-reinforced fiberglass Ornaments of hand-applied gold leaf and mirror mosaic, featuring rich gold braid, beading, jewels, and holographic detailing.

7 MGM GRAND DETROIT, DETROIT, MICHIGAN

Striking nine-foot square Wreath featuring sculpted synthetic glass ribbon finished in hand-applied gold leaf.

8 GAYLORD NATIONAL HOTEL, WASHINGTON, DC

Suspended 30 feet from the floor is a 60-foot Holiday Tree of synthetic glass Holly leaves trimmed with 8-foot berry sprays and topped with bow and cascading ribbon of synthetic glass, hand-sculpted and finished in hand-applied gold leaf. Directly under the tree a giant gift box directs light upward into the tree, illuminating the translucent green boughs.

9-10 ROCKEFELLER CENTER, NEW YORK, NEW YORK

32-foot stack of Claes Oldenburg-inspired 8-foot diameter Holiday Ornaments appear to float in block-long reflecting pool in front of Radio City Music Hall.

11 WACHOVIA BANK, CHARLOTTE, NORTH CAROLINA

48-foot Holiday Tree with custom ornamentation of hand-applied gold leaf Acanthus leaves and gold and red glass ornaments, stands in a custom-designed base adorned with hand-sculpted dimensional fiberglass Della Robbia garlands finished in gold leaf. The ornaments suspended overhead range in size from 8 to 12 feet and are finished in gold leaf, red velvet upholstery, gold braid, beading, jewels and rope lighting. 8 and 12-foot Millennium stars are finished in gold glitter.

12 222 BERKELEY, BOSTON, MASSACHUSETTS

13-foot steel-reinforced fiberglass Holiday Bells with hand-sculpted and gold-leafed details and bright red flocking are suspended from quilted red holiday ribbon.

13 UPPER LEFT: PLUS CITY, LINZ, AUSTRIA

Custom 8-foot to 18-foot Ornaments upholstered in red velvet and finished with hand-applied gold leaf, jewels, and mirror mosaic tiles.

LOWER LEFT: TRAMMEL CROW CENTER, DALLAS, TEXAS

14th-Century Italian Renaissance Angel with 18-foot wingspan holding a golden trumpet. Costuming is created in wired Dupione silk, and hair of sculpted sisal. Vatican doves of sculpted papier-mâché trail clouds of white silk.

UPPER CENTER: TANDY CENTER, FT. WORTH, TEXAS

Gold-leafed 5-pointed fiberglass Stars in descending sizes are suspended within an 8-story atrium.

LOWER CENTER: SONY WORLD MUSIC HEADQUARTERS, NEW YORK, NEW YORK

45-foot hand-sculpted Bow with steel armature finished in red flocking and hand-applied gold leaf.

UPPER RIGHT: AMERICAN EXPRESS BUILDING, NEW YORK, NEW YORK

19-foot Banners with hand-painted murals depicting Christmas around the world. Banners are trimmed with three-dimensional Della Robbia garlands in hand-applied gold leaf.

LOWER RIGHT: TRUMP TOWER, NEW YORK, NEW YORK

12-foot double-sided Wreath was suspended from glass façade with bow and streamers of papier maché on steel, finished in hand-applied gold leaf. Decor on the wreath includes oversize gemstones lit from within.

14 JP MORGAN CHASE, SAN FRANCISCO, CALIFORNIA

Giant Claes Oldenburg-inspired Sleigh Bells strung on steel-reinforced red velvet ribbon "float" in the lobby of the corporate headquarters for JP Morgan Chase.

15-16 BELLAGIO, LAS VEGAS, NEVADA

Left: 19th-Century Canadian Sleigh adorned with gold leaf striping, jewels and Venetian-cut mirror, upholstered in Christmas red velvet. Nestled in its lush white 'fur' sleigh rug are gift boxes of mirror mosaic tile and gold ribbon.

Center: Reindeer of hand-applied pecans in full flight above a towering stack of gift boxes in mirror mosaic tile with red ribbon, gold-leaf and red velvet ornaments richly decorated in mirror mosaic tile, gold braid and jewels, and a 12-foot Hobby Horse.

Right: Detail of giant hand-painted Hobby Horse with hand-applied gold leaf saddle and striping, and trim of mirror pavé.

17 LEFT: AMERICAN EXPRESS WORLD HEADQUARTERS, NEW YORK, NEW YORK

14-foot Wreath trimmed in winter foliage and lush ornamentation. The ribbon is of hand sculpted steel-reinforced fiberglass finished in hand-applied gold leaf.

RIGHT: AT&T CORPORATE OFFICES, CHICAGO, ILLINOIS

28-foot swag of winter foliage with lavish custom ornamentation. Hand-sculpted steel-reinforced fiberglass end caps are finished in hand-applied gold leaf.

18 ROCKEFELLER CENTER, NEW YORK, NEW YORK

Left: Norman Rockwell-inspired Holiday Cadets at Rockefeller Center are dressed in uniforms to match the Center's international flag display. The cadets flank the skating rink and Christmas tree above the Prometheus statue.

Center: Rockefeller Tree topped with a Millennium Star of steel-reinforced fiberglass finished in hand-applied gold leaf.

Right: The inspiration for these toy soldiers came from the original series that Mr. Rockwell created for the Boy Scouts of America.

19 FASHION SHOW MALL, LAS VEGAS, NEVADA

Lavishly costumed, hand-painted Erté-Inspired figures complement each 8-foot Holiday Ornament forming the "dress" of the figure. The "ornament dress" is upholstered in red velvet and ornamented with jewels, beads, giant "pearls," feathers and gold leaf accents. Overall height 19 feet. The mannequins, custom-sculpted in London, each wear a rich silk or satin headdress adorned with feathers, jewels, and beads. Design Solutions holds a world-wide license from the Erté estate to reproduce his designs as holiday décor.

20 FASHION SHOW MALL, LAS VEGAS, NEVADA

Upper Left: Two 12-foot figures dressed in red gowns and connected by opulent red sashes stand on mirrored bases. The inspiration for the statuesque "Twins" was a 1930's era Harper's Bazaar cover designed by Erté.

Center Left: Exquisite Erté-inspired figure costumed in white satin, gold and silver; her lavish holiday headdress is adorned with wired pearls and feathers to create an exotic fantasy.

Lower Left: Reclining figure in a 12-foot jeweled silver wreath balances a clear snow globe in her hand. The figure was inspired by a 1930's advertisement for Courvoisier.

Right: Lalique-Inspired Holiday Tree, formed of frosted and etched synthetic glass light boxes with snowflake panels created in the style of world-renown glass artist René Lalique. The Tree is topped with a 6-foot "snowburst," of synthetic glass encrusted with hand-applied "ice" chips and sparkling with computer-animated LED interior lighting

21 BELLAGIO, LAS VEGAS, NEVADA

The 50-foot "Tiara Tree," constructed of a hand-wrought steel armature, beaded in red and silver and traced in rope lights with mirrored medallions, was inspired by a chandelier in the new Bellagio Spa Tower. The "Tiara" sits over a fresh-cut 50-foot fir tree illuminated by thousands of red LED lights, and is topped with an 8-foot red mirror pavé Millennium Star. It is surrounded by 12- and 18-foot mirrored mosaic Millennium stars suspended from the conservatory ceiling. At its base sit giant ornaments of hand-applied gold leaf, red velvet, gold rope beads and jewels.

22 LENOX SQUARE, ATLANTA, GEORGIA

The installation in Atlanta, Georgia for Lenox Square Mall won both national and international awards. Flanking the entrance, two 16-foot square wreaths are capped with sculpted frozen snow; whimsical mirrored stars replicate billboard advertising for the property. The rooftop light show included thirteen 10,000-watt Synchrolite animated beams. Millennium star designs are constructed of steel and animated with computerized lighting. Every 30 minutes offered a spectacular light show with a live radio simulcast of original music composed for the project.

23 BELLAGIO, LAS VEGAS, NEVADA – RETAIL

Left: Stylish mannequin attired in a lavish holiday gown is seated atop an 8-foot ornament of steel-reinforced fiberglass with hand-applied gold leaf. Custom wigs and makeup complete the "look" of each mannequin. The festive gowns are embellished with jewels, fur, feathers and sequins. Shoes are by Manolo Blahnik.

Right: 45-foot Holiday Ball Tree formed of 5-, 4-, and 3-foot ornaments of hand-applied gold leaf, supporting seated life-size mannequin costumed as above. The mannequin at left wears a feather boa and stands atop an 8-foot steel-reinforced fiberglass ornament finished in hand-applied gold-leaf.

24 BOSTON PROPERTIES / PRUDENTIAL CENTER, BOSTON, MASSACHUSETTS

Left: Striking 8-and 12-foot Millennium Holiday Stars finished in hand-applied gold leaf are suspended from the atrium ceiling against backdrop of a 30-foot double-sided Holiday Wreath.

Right: Night view of the 30-foot double-sided Wreath adorned with giant custom-sculpted Acanthus leaves finished in hand-applied gold leaf, and large-scale red and gold custom ornamentation.

SPRING

25-26 MGM GRAND DETROIT, DETROIT, MICHIGAN

Detail of giant hand-sculpted synthetic glass Parrot Tulip against deep blue sky.

27 MGM GRAND DETROIT, DETROIT, MICHIGAN

This Claes Oldenburg-inspired montage created an outdoor must-see destination garden, here shown at night in dramatic lighting.

28 MGM GRAND DETROIT, DETROIT, MICHIGAN

The 18-foot fiberglass pot with faux terra-cotta finish holds 43-foot synthetic glass Parrot Tulips and foliage. The 27-foot sculpted trowel is cantilevered with a custom steel armature and underground foundation.

29 BELLAGIO, LAS VEGAS, NEVADA

Detail of synthetic glass Poppies showing accurate representation of poppy stamens created of silk petals on custom steel "arms" flocked in flat black.

30 BELLAGIO, LAS VEGAS, NEVADA

18-foot California Poppies custom sculpted in hand-painted synthetic glass are growing from steel pipe stems with leaves of custom-sculpted foam on steel armatures, all air-brushed to closely mimic nature. The buds and calyxes are similarly constructed. The surrounding butterflies are steel and mesh forms covered in dried flowers and seeds.

31 BELLAGIO, LAS VEGAS, NEVADA

Left and Upper Right: The "Ruins" were inspired by the film *The Secret Garden,* and are custom sculpted of steel reinforced stone with concrete coating and theatrical painting, finished with accents of live Pennsylvania clump moss.

Lower Right: Custom topiary Snail is covered in 9,000 colored roses with sculpted head and antennae covered in dried mushrooms and seeds.

32 BELLAGIO, LAS VEGAS, NEVADA

37-foot Palladian-styled Temple of Love crafted after the original located at the Palace of Versailles in France, a gift of Louis XIV to Marie Antoinette. The Temple measures 20 feet in diameter and is filled with 15,000 live butterflies. The room is alive with swarms of translucent, articulated silk butterflies flying in "laminar flow."

33 BELLAGIO, LAS VEGAS, NEVADA - RETAIL

6- and 8-foot diameter hand-painted tulip-theme Umbrellas float from overhead among lush planters whose live foliage is enhanced with swarms of silk butterflies.

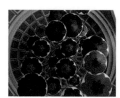

34 BELLAGIO, LAS VEGAS, NEVADA - RETAIL

A profusion of Umbrellas cascade from the dome ceiling. The Umbrellas are hand-painted from photos of open tulips and are suspended from resin handles crafted to mimic bamboo.

35 BELLAGIO, LAS VEGAS, NEVADA

Two stately Egrets, covered in down and white statice, stand in a pond with giant synthetic glass lotus blossoms and buds. 16-foot butterflies of steel frames covered in flowers fly above the custom English greenhouse which is filled with 15,000 live butterflies.

36 BELLAGIO, LAS VEGAS, NEVADA

Spring Tulip display is mirrored in 30" reflection fountain sphere. Each bed of raised waddle fencing creates the design for a French Garden. A Japanese Garden behind is created from raked granite gravel, rare TaiHu rock raised specimens and a custom bamboo tea house.

37 BELLAGIO, LAS VEGAS, NEVADA

Left: A fascinating ant colony thrives in the Conservatory Gardens, sculpted in monumental proportions and anatomical detail by American artist, Susan P. Cochran. These bronze works of art create a fantasy wonderland for the Spring season.

Right: Here we see an ant attracted to an overturned 15-foot flowerpot spilling cascades of seasonal blooms. An enormous 28-foot hand spade is staked alongside, waiting to assist with the next garden project. Butterflies and bees hover overhead alongside the joyful yellow jonquils.

38 BELLAGIO, LAS VEGAS, NEVADA

Giant mushrooms, ranging from 5 to 15 ft. in height offer wonderful natural canopies for the frogs, ants and other critters in the garden. Two 6' 9" ants battle playfully near a cascading leaf fountain where rain water trickles down to replenish a fresh-water pond.

39-40 BELLAGIO, LAS VEGAS, NEVADA

Giant Watering Cans were inspired by an exhibition garden in Chamont, France. The 5 - 1/2 foot cans were hand made of galvanized tin with solid copper details. Fountains of water pour from the cans onto summer foliage planted in the gardens below. Colorful flowers burst from outsize hand-painted fantasy pots.

SUMMER

41-42 BELLAGIO, LAS VEGAS, NEVADA

45-foot 1949 Ferris Wheel brightly refurbished in Spring green, yellow and orange, decorative metal custom appliqués, and computer animated carnival lights. Glossy red vinyl seats overflow with brilliant sunflowers. The center of the wheel features a hand-sculpted sunflower bearing the Bellagio "B" logo. Hand-painted Hot-air Balloons are suspended from the atrium ceiling, each containing a small fan to keep it aloft. The Corvette was on loan from the Corvette museum in Bowling Green, Kentucky, and was used in the 1960-64 television series "Route 66."

43 BELLAGIO, LAS VEGAS, NEVADA

Left: Detail of Hot-air Balloon showing custom-painted cloud scene; Ferris Wheel detail with sunflower and Bellagio logo.

Right: Glossy Red Carnival Seats spill bright sunflowers.

44 BELLAGIO, LAS VEGAS, NEVADA

Left: Preserved Monarch Butterflies on wire armature are entwined in live foliage vining on trellis.

Right: Giant 5-1/2 foot Watering Can of galvanized tin and copper, spraying flowers planted in hand-painted Fantasy Pot.

45 BELLAGIO, LAS VEGAS, NEVADA

A 33-foot wide topiary American Eagle covered in leaves, seeds, and natural materials clutches gold-leafed arrows and laurel branches. He hovers above a 16-foot exact replica of the Liberty Bell in Philadelphia, finished in powdered bronze. 13 hand-applied gold leaf stars fly above the composition, and animated 6-foot laminar fountains dance through the garden below.

46 BELLAGIO, LAS VEGAS, NEVADA

Spectacular reproduction of the Bellagio, Las Vegas, in twig, seeds and natural materials in front of an overhead trellis bridge constructed of willow twigs. The garden-scale train rushes by in the foreground.

47 BELLAGIO, LAS VEGAS, NEVADA

Garden-scale train crosses willow-twig trellis bridge in front of the hand-sculpted reproduction of Mt. Rushmore.

48 BELLAGIO, LAS VEGAS, NEVADA

This scene shows the detailed, to-scale replica of the Washington Monument and the reflecting pool leading to the Lincoln Memorial. The intricate overhead trellis bridge is of willow twigs.

49 BELLAGIO, LAS VEGAS, NEVADA

This cheerful topiary girl is costumed in live floral displays. Her dog is created of seeds and rice.

50 BELLAGIO, LAS VEGAS, NEVADA

The Huck Finn-like figure was inspired by a Norman Rockwell painting of children fishing. The figure is created in fresh flowers, statice and dried materials. The boat and basket are of bark and natural materials.

AUTUMN

51-52 BELLAGIO CONSERVATORY, LAS VEGAS, NEVADA

The 38-foot New England-style Cider Mill is constructed of fieldstone and barnwood with an operating water wheel. A 50-foot animated talking tree sits to the right in a garden of live flowers, topped with brilliant fall foliage. The tree's mouth, eyes, and face move as it welcomes the guests.

53 BELLAGIO, LAS VEGAS, NEVADA

Left: Intricate "Raintrees" sculpted of copper pipe and leaves with water spraying from each leaf and spilling into the pond below. In the background a giant wooden tub spills a colorful river of fresh apples.

Right: Detail of Copper Fountain Tree

54 BELLAGIO, LAS VEGAS, NEVADA

The giant 12-foot papier-maché Tree Troll (Ent) sculpture is a friendly visitor to the Fall Garden. His vivid blue eyes and bittersweet vining accent his magical presence.

55 MGM GRAND DETROIT, DETROIT, MICHIGAN

Sun streaming through a giant 27-foot red synthetic glass Oak leaf mounted on a 50-foot armature, against a forest of Canadian Birch trees hand-selected and grown for Design Solutions.

56 MGM GRAND DETROIT, DETROIT, MICHIGAN

The sun casts a bright red shadow through the giant Oak Leaf onto the MGM Grand façade.

57 MGM GRAND DETROIT, DETROIT, MICHIGAN

Against the backdrop of a 50-foot Birch forest in front of the MGM Grand Façade, autumn leaves seem to float in the air over the garden of 700 lb. to1,500 lb. giant pumpkins and squash. Custom architectural lighting throughout the garden makes for an enchanted evening setting.

58 MGM GRAND DETROIT, DETROIT, MICHIGAN

50-foot Birch forest forms a stunning autumn backdrop to the 27-foot, hand-sculpted and painted synthetic glass leaves. The leaves cast vivid, colorful shadows as the sun moves across the sky.

59 BELLAGIO, LAS VEGAS, NEVADA

Stunning, free-floating topiary Canadian Mallard Ducks emerge from a giant topiary painting of live plants and dried floral materials. You can see the Mallards reflected in the waterway below.

60 BELLAGIO, LAS VEGAS, NEVADA

Americana Covered Bridge with roof of mushrooms and fungi. Sculpted leaf fountain spills water into the stream below, while giant synthetic glass leaves drift overhead.

61 BELLAGIO, LAS VEGAS, NEVADA

Left: Detail of topiary Table & Chairs with Chandelier overhead

Center: Detail of Succulents

Right: Closeup of Chair and Table

62 BELLAGIO, LAS VEGAS, NEVADA

Fantasy Secret Garden with walls of living moss, topiary chairs and table of live succulents, and overhead chandelier spilling cut orchid stems.

WINTER

63-64 MGM GRAND DETROIT, DETROIT, MICHIGAN

14-foot Caribou graze in front of a 50' Birch forest sparkling with tiny white LED lights. Their iridescent coats reflect a light show of changing colors, offering a riveting, never-ending display. The 28-foot "icebursts" of synthetic glass are mounted on steel poles and sparkle with internal light synchronized with the colors bathing the Caribou.

65 MGM GRAND DETROIT, DETROIT, MICHIGAN

As the sky darkens into evening, the winter scene of grazing Caribou against the 50' Birch forest is bathed in a constant light show ranging in spectrum from blue through purple, pink, red, to yellow.

66 MGM GRAND DETROIT, DETROIT, MICHIGAN

A lone Caribou grazeing with the setting sun streaming through its translucent coat shows in detail the striking change of color as the sun sets and night comes on.

67 PLUS CITY, LINZ, AUSTRIA

A profusion of 28-foot "icebursts," suspended from the atrium ceiling, are crafted of hand-sculpted synthetic glass and adorned with hundreds of hand-applied "ice" chips to reflect the light.

68 PLUS CITY, LINZ, AUSTRIA

Giant 12 to 18-foot "icebursts" of synthetic glass are suspended from the atrium ceiling in the Plus City Mall. The icebursts are accented with hundreds of tiny ice chips that sparkle in the light.

69 LEFT: EQUITIBLE LIFE, NEW YORK, NEW YORK

12-foot custom-sculpted Pine Cones, gilded and glittered with intense theatrical lighting, are suspended from dimensional velvet ribbons.

RIGHT: 101 SECOND STREET / HINES INTERESTS, SAN FRANCISCO, CALIFORNIA

6-foot Pine Cones are finished in striking gold and glitter and suspended from hand-channel-quilted red velvet ribbons.

70 101 SECOND STREET / HINES INTERESTS, SAN FRANCISCO, CALIFORNIA

Dramatic view of the Pine Cones from below show their true beauty and scale.

71 BELLAGIO, LAS VEGAS, NEVADA

Detail of Snow "Mom" showing custom-designed and hand-sewn clothing of all-natural elements including feathers, seeds, nuts, and berries.

72 BELLAGIO, LAS VEGAS, NEVADA

Topiary Snow Family of white carnations, in hand-crafted clothing of seeds, berries and all-natural components. Peppermint sticks are hand-painted and glazed to look like sugar delights. To the right, an 18-foot iceburst glitters with interior LED lights.

73 BELLAGIO, LAS VEGAS, NEVADA

Animated adult and baby Penguins stand atop hand-sculpted and painted icebergs in front of frozen "ice" tree. Overhead "icebursts" are sculpted of synthetic glass and accented with thousands of tiny chips of acrylic ice.

74 BELLAGIO, LAS VEGAS, NEVADA

Topiary Polar Bears covered in 80,000 white carnations wear scarves crafted from brilliant red mosaic mirror tiles. The bridge is of real birch logs, and "icebursts" sparkle overhead.

CHINESE NEW YEAR

75-76 BELLAGIO. LAS VEGAS, NEVADA

Live floral topiary Children on bridge with hand-sculpted, hand-painted faces and hands, clothed in silk adorned with flowers, seeds and berries. Large, custom silk Chinese lanterns hang suspended from the atrium ceiling. The hand-painted God of Fortune is clothed in authentic Oriental fabrics; his gold brocade jacket is trimmed in faux fur. The 150-foot Banyan Tree to the right was moved from The Four Arts Museum in Palm Beach, Florida in sections and re-assembled in the Conservatory.

77 BELLAGIO, LAS VEGAS, NEVADA

The imposing sculpted God of Prosperity stands upon a mountain of golden I-Ching coins in shoes of hand-applied gold leaf.

78 BELLAGIO, LAS VEGAS, NEVADA

Left: 30-foot Chinoiserie Pagoda of red lacquer with gold leaf accents and green-glazed tile roof was custom-crafted from European studies.

Right: The lifelike Ram celebrates the Chinese Year of the Ram.

79 BELLAGIO, LAS VEGAS, NEVADA

18-foot red silk Chinese Pagoda Lantern with hand-made tassel and gold leaf calligraphy appropriate to the year. The Lantern to the right is of red silk and velvet with a custom Chinese knot holding the hand-made tassel.

80 BELLAGIO, LAS VEGAS, NEVADA

Live floral topiary Children play beneath 88-foot strand of Giant Firecrackers enscribed with gold leaf Chinese calligraphy.

81 BELLAGIO, LAS VEGAS, NEVADA

Left: Live floral topiary Chinese child plays with Bamboo stick

Right: Three topiary Children in garden

82 BELLAGIO, LAS VEGAS, NEVADA

Imposing Chinese wall element with moon gate and glazed tile roof. Black bamboo specimens with rare TaiHu Scholar's stone in foreground.

83 BELLAGIO, LAS VEGAS, NEVADA

A beautiful, wing-tipped Ming Dynasty-styled gazebo is the ultimate destination for the red-laquered zig-zag bridge traversing the main garden. It is believed that a zig-zag bridge focuses the pedestrian's attention to the current place and time; the design also follows a principle of *Feng Shui*, assuming negative energy and bad spirits have problems navigating corners, while people and good energy do not. Adjacent to the Ming-styled gazebo is a tranquil Koi pond--another very auspicious element for Chinese New Year where koi appear in multiples of the lucky number eight.

84 BELLAGIO, LAS VEGAS, NEVADA

Exquisite 11-foot Tang Dynasty Horse covered in mirror mosaic pavé, with hand-applied gold-leaf accents, saddle and trim.

OLYMPICS 2010

85&86 WINTER OLYMPICS 2010, VANCOUVER, BC, CANADA

The City of Richmond, BC is home to the Richmond Olympic Oval, a 47,526 square metre indoor competition venue for the Vancouver 2010 Olympic and Paralympic Winter Games. Design Solutions was asked to provide an installation for the City of Richmond celebrating the Olympic theme. The result, complete with Ferris Wheel for panoramic views, can be seen in this evening photograph taken from Richmond City Hall.

87 WINTER OLYMPICS 2010, VANCOUVER, BC, CANADA

Gold-leafing of the Olympic Flame; delivery, pre-assembly and staging of the giant display at McDonald Beach in Richmond.

88 WINTER OLYMPICS 2010, VANCOUVER, BC, CANADA

Construction and installation of the 46,000 sq. ft. floating cranberry bog at the O Zone, the Olympic celebration site for the City of Richmond.

89 WINTER OLYMPICS 2010, VANCOUVER, BC, CANADA

Panoramic view of giant cranberry "bogs" celebrating the 2010 Winter Olympics.

90 WINTER OLYMPICS 2010, VANCOUVER, BC, CANADA

Stephen Stefanou, President and Design Director of Design Solutions at the culmination of the six-month project created for Ocean Spray and the City of Richmond.

99 BELLAGIO, LAS VEGAS, NEVADA

19-foot Crystal Obelisk produced of white quartz crystal by Zadora of London. Permanent installation.